DOGS SET V

Bichons Frises

Julie Murray
ABDO Publishing Company

visit us at
www.abdopub.com

Published by ABDO Publishing Company, 4940 Viking Drive, Edina, Minnesota 55435.
Copyright © 2003 by Abdo Consulting Group, Inc. International copyrights reserved in
all countries. No part of this book may be reproduced in any form without written
permission from the publisher.

Printed in the United States.

Cover Photo: Ron Kimball
Interior Photos: Animals Animals pp. 9, 11, 17, 21; Corbis pp. 5, 7, 13, 19;
   Ron Kimball p. 15

Contributing Editors: Kate A. Conley, Kristin Van Cleaf, Kristianne E. Vieregger
Art Direction & Graphics: Neil Klinepier

Library of Congress Cataloging-in-Publication Data

Murray, Julie, 1969-
   Bichons frises / Julie Murray.
     p. cm. -- (Dogs Set V)
   Summary: An introduction to the physical characteristics, behavior, and proper care
of Bichons Frises.
   Includes bibliographical references (p.).
   ISBN 1-57765-921-X
    1. Bichon frise--Juvenile literature. [1. Bichon frise. 2. Dogs.] I. Title.

SF429.B52 M87 2003
636.72--dc21

                                   2002074653

Contents

The Dog Family

Dogs and humans have been living together for thousands of years. Dogs were first tamed about 12,000 years ago. They were used as guards, hunters, and companions.

Today, about 400 different dog **breeds** exist. They can differ greatly in appearance. Some can weigh as much as 200 pounds (91 kg). Others are small enough to fit in the palms of your hands.

Despite these differences, all dogs belong to the same scientific **family**. It is called Canidae. The name comes from the Latin word *canis*, which means dog.

The Canidae family includes more than just **domestic** dogs. Foxes, jackals, coyotes, and wolves belong to the Canidae family, too. In fact, many people believe today's domestic dogs descended from wolves.

Bichons frises are related to other animals in the Canidae family, such as the wolf.

Bichons Frises

The exact history of bichons frises is uncertain. However, it is known that four **breeds** of bichons originated in the Mediterranean area. They are the bichon maltais, the bichon havanais, the bichon bolognais, and the bichon teneriffe. Today, the teneriffe is known as the bichon frise.

In the 1500s, bichons frises were popular with European royalty. In the late 1800s, bichons frises performed in European circuses. They could jump very high, walk on their hind legs, and even do somersaults.

In 1956, Helen and François Picualt of France brought bichons frises to the United States. The breed was recognized by the **American Kennel Club** in 1973.

A bichon frise

What They're Like

Bichons frises make wonderful family pets. They are happy, playful, and intelligent. They get along well with children and with other pets. Bichons are even friendly with cats.

Bichons frises need lots of love and attention. They will follow you around the house and sit by your side or on your lap. These dogs do not like to be left alone for long periods of time.

Bichons frises are quiet, passive dogs. However, they will bark to warn their owners if something is wrong. Bichons frises are easy to train. They are sensitive dogs that learn quickly.

Opposite page: Bichons enjoy exploring the outdoors.

Coat and Color

A bichon frise has a white, powder-puff appearance. Its outercoat is coarse with corkscrew curls. The undercoat is soft and **dense**. The whole coat feels soft and silky, almost like velvet. The bichon's coat does not shed.

A bichon's coat is white. A bichon frise puppy can sometimes be born with cream or apricot shadings on its coat. These colors usually disappear by the time the puppy is full grown. But sometimes an adult bichon will have cream, buff, or apricot shadings around its ears.

Opposite page: The bichon frise's coat gives the breed its distinctive appearance.

Size

The bichon frise is a small, compact dog. The **breed** stands between 9 and 12 inches (23 and 30 cm) tall at the shoulders. A bichon usually only weighs between 7 and 12 pounds (3 and 5 kg). A female bichon is normally a bit smaller than a male.

The bichon has a **unique** body. It has a long, arched neck. Its **plumed** tail curves over its back. This allows the tail's hair to rest on the dog's back. The bichon has dark, round eyes surrounded by dark rims. Its nose and lips are black.

Opposite page: The bichon's small size makes it a good pet for people who live in apartments or small houses.

Care

The bichon frise takes lots of work to be groomed properly. It needs regular bathing, brushing, and trimming to maintain its beautiful powder-puff coat.

Before bathing your bichon, use a pin brush to remove all the matted areas on its coat. After the bath, it's time to style your bichon's coat. To do this, use a hair dryer and pin brush. This will give your dog the true bichon look.

Like any dog, the bichon frise needs to visit the **veterinarian** at least once a year for a checkup. The veterinarian can check your dog for illnesses and give it shots to prevent diseases. If you are not going to **breed** your dog, have the veterinarian **spay** or **neuter** it.

It's a good idea to take your bichon to a professional groomer every two to three months.

Feeding

Bichons enjoy routines, especially when it comes to feeding. They like to eat at the same time every day. Bichons should be fed only once a day.

Dog food can be dry, moist, or semimoist. Most bichons will eat a high-quality, dry dog food. Others prefer to have some canned food mixed in with their dry food.

Find a type of dog food that your dog enjoys and stick with it. Changes in diet should be done gradually to prevent stomach problems. It is also important to give your dog fresh, clean water every day.

Opposite page: Bichon puppies should be fed four times a day. When they are older, they only need one meal a day.

Things They Need

A bichon frise needs love and human contact to be happy. It needs space to run and play and enjoys a walk every day. Like any dog, the bichon frise needs a quiet place to rest in your house. It also needs something comfortable to lie on. A dog bed or soft blanket works well for this.

The bichon frise does poorly in hot temperatures. When it is hot, walk your bichon in the early morning or late evening. When the weather is cool, the bichon's furry coat keeps it warm. So walking your bichon during the winter months is not a problem.

Every dog should wear a collar with two tags. One tag shows the dog has had its shots. The other tag shows the dog's name and its owner's address and phone number. A dog can also have a **tattoo** or **microchip** for identification.

Bichons do best when they have lots of human attention.

Puppies

Baby dogs are called puppies. A mother dog is **pregnant** for about nine weeks. Bichons frises have about three to five puppies in a **litter**.

Puppies are born blind and deaf. Their eyes and ears will begin working when they are about two weeks old. They can walk at three weeks, and they are usually **weaned** at about seven weeks of age.

Puppies can be given away or sold when they are about eight weeks old. If you are going to buy a **purebred** puppy, make sure to buy it from a qualified **breeder**. Many puppies and older dogs are also available from the **Humane Society**.

It is important to take your puppy to the **veterinarian**. He or she will give your puppy the shots it needs to stay healthy. A puppy should start getting its shots when it is between six and eight weeks old. A healthy bichon frise will live 15 to 16 years.

A bichon frise puppy

Glossary

American Kennel Club - a club that studies, breeds, and exhibits purebred dogs.

breed - a group of dogs sharing the same appearance and characteristics. A breeder is a person who raises dogs. Raising dogs is often called breeding them.

dense - thick.

domestic - living with humans.

family - a group that scientists use to classify similar plants and animals. It ranks above a genus and below an order.

Humane Society - an organization that cares for and protects animals.

litter - all the puppies born at one time to a mother dog.

microchip - a small computer chip. A veterinarian inserts the chip between a dog's shoulder blades. If the dog is lost, the Humane Society can scan the chip to find the dog's identification information and owners.

neuter - to remove a male animal's reproductive parts.

plume - a large, fluffy feather or something that resembles one.

pregnant - having one or more babies growing within the body.

purebred - an animal whose parents are both from the same breed.

spay - to remove a female animal's reproductive parts.

tattoo - a permanent design made on the skin. An owner can have an identification number tattooed on the leg of his or her dog.

unique - different from any other.

veterinarian - a doctor who cares for animals.

wean - to accustom an animal to eating food other than its mother's milk.

Web Sites

Would you like to learn more about bichons frises? Please visit **www.abdopub.com** to find up-to-date Web site links about dog care and the bichon frise breed. These links are routinely monitored and updated to provide the most current information available.

Index